I0224676

Evanescent

Poems

by

Maria-Cristina Necula

Finishing Line Press
Georgetown, Kentucky

Evanescent

Poems

Publisher: Leah Huete de Maines
Editor: Christen Kincaid
Cover Art: Maria-Cristina Necula
Author Photo: Jorge Madrigal
Cover Design: Elizabeth Maines McCleavy

Order online: www.finishinglinepress.com
also available on amazon.com

Author inquiries and mail orders:
Finishing Line Press
P. O. Box 1626
Georgetown, Kentucky 40324
U. S. A.

Table of Contents

In loving memory of my grandparents:
Diancu, Elisabeta, Nicolae, and Svetlana

Timely Argument

I had an argument with time.
It cost me half a decade
of counting yesterdays,
but I have never spent
a second
on my cursed lament
of living sooner
than the Chronos intent.

Word-Made

I had a dream that I was made of words,
from head to toe, a body built by sentences and paragraphs,
coherent and absurd,
entirely dependent on the letters,
for their arrangements
rendered magic to my flesh.

If you could read me limb by limb
and cell by cell,
and every foreign term of my construction learn to spell,
you'd turn this dictionary of exhausting contradictions
into your own encyclopedia
of tender definitions.

The Hands of Blue Time United

The hands of blue time united
into the mast of a sailboat.
And I was captain on that deck of shadows,
at the helm, I too a shadow
resisting impermanence,
asking, is all or any of it real
or am I writing myself into a mystery?
Either way I'd never want to miss
one second
of the unsettling wonder
of It all.

there and here

the sky opened
into a million fragments that resembled universes
and took me into a dream
in which you appeared every place
and every time at once
and I was no longer certain
whether that was me or you
or me dreaming inside a dream of seeing you
there and here
and everywhere
in your unfettered presence
among those diamond celestial specks
those pieces of the mirrors of eternity
there and here where no displacement is possible
because there and here and yesterday and tomorrow
happen on the same breath
and you exist in all

Vision

inside a teardrop
I saw the map
the soul's geography
in salty waters drowned
a microscopic universe
of pain
unbound

Wooing Woes

Destiny woos
the hand of Time
not by gentleness
or bourgeois manners
but through a livid rendition
of domination gone awry
presenting certificates of authenticity
torn from tattered astrology books
birthdates and charts
certificate upon certificate
Destiny of numbers seasons planets
controlling what we know and fear and wish we can control

Time has no time
for numbered courtship
and Destiny as a displeased deluded lover
falters in the aftermath of calculation

Time refuses collaboration

until the Mind can blur the numbers
of the perfect
match

In Bliss

If Kundalini called my name
I would not know to answer
for at last she holds
my cells
in bliss
of deconstruction

Woman of Shadows

I stand raw,
I lie sacred,
I've pressed all your buttons
To summon truth naked.

Dare to try
And let your instincts fly,
Can you feel
The devil at your heel?

I'm the woman of shadows,
Standing right behind you,
Don't slip, don't slide, don't cower,
One move and I surround you.

I lurk in every doubt,
I lure you to impasse,
I'm crawling through your veins
With a magnifying glass.

Drop your weapons,
You're no angel.
"Cowards die a thousand deaths"
And you're in danger.

Routine saves you
Till daylight disappears,
I'm the darkest midnight
Of your deepest fears.

I'm dancing on your conscience
As you're digging your own hole,
Open your mind, stranger,
I'm the mirror to your soul.

Who Can?

I can't fit in!
I can't fit in!
Said the spirit to the skin.

I can't conform!
I can't conform!
Said the rebel to the norm.

I can't comply!
I can't comply!
Said the tongue to the white lie.

I can't resist!
I can't resist!
Said the sinner to the priest.

I can't pretend!
I can't pretend!
Said the artist to the trend.

I can't sustain!
I can't sustain!
Said the neuron to the pain.

I can't be sold!
I can't be sold!
Said the honor to the gold.

I can't forget!
I can't forget!
Said the heartache to regret.

I can't control!
I can't control!
Said the star to the black hole.

I can't refuse!

I can't refuse!
Said the yenta to the news.

I can't escape!
I can't escape!
Said the man's genes to the ape.

I can't command!
I can't command!
Said the hourglass to the sand.

I can't correct!
I can't correct!
Said the cause to the effect.

I can't reply!
I can't reply!
Said the echo to the cry.

I can't return!
I can't return!
Said the ashes to the urn.

I can't say 'no'!
I can't say 'no'!
Said the mistress to her glow.

I can't be wise!
I can't be wise!
Said the longing to the eyes.

I can't be caught!
I can't be caught!
Said the instinct to the thought.

I can't be me!
I can't be me!
Said I to my memory.

compass

this floating psyche has been pulverized
I anchor it through consonants and vowels
I pull my mind—the phantom ship—at bay
with ropes of words woven into sentences

my pen my compass

soul mind dissolved
scattering shapes
deleting data
convulsions of the Self
now searching for refuge in something solid
withdrawing into bones
stuffing itSelf inside tendons muscles tissues
crying save me save me
from the emptiness out there
from the freedom out there

for Self is terrorized by infinity
it hides it hides
until bones ache and tendons strain and muscles cramp
and this unique mortal carcass is a shelter of pain
self-destructing by violent longing to contain its truth

because the eyes see
and the mind knows the familiar flashes
glimpses of past present future colliding into one
all in one instant
all consuming
all too burdensome and wondrous
responsibility to know
to see

and clinging to my pen
within the terrifying space of this limitless now
I sketch a path of term-less ink across the border
of an unchartered me

Photodream

I dreamt I was a photograph
of your dance with the infinite
watching you paint distinction
with equality

humans fabricated in the factory of divine will
one by one
claim eternity
at the gates of your perception

your eyes trace patterns
of misery and decadence
inside a tender cosmic space

you grasp
the circle of a moment
uncovering its perfect form

for through the lens
your eyes
hold the promise of truth

Suburban Neighbors

The cars line up
the parking lot
in a geometrical attempt
to measure and protect
suburban congruity,
while the scorched bed
in apartment 10
conceals
inside its glowing embers
a somewhat
neighborly
ambiguity.

Impossibility

I find it difficult to give
when you ask
my love to be
a task.

An ancient allergy erupts
when you fill the air
with constancy perfume
and care.

You love me and I tell myself
the privilege is mine.
Your love is strong
like cellar-dwelling wine.

You ask if I still like you
in a 5:00am bout
of sensitivity.
You doubt.

In my adult version
of Show-and-Tell, I'm proud
to be loved by you
in a crowd.

But I am just a loner
who belongs to a strange race
in love
with space.

My Lovers Don't Complain

My lovers don't complain
but they enumerate
the qualities of Woman
I've come to wear
as long-debated garments

My lovers don't complain
but they demand
their definitions met and no rebellion
perturb their sense of
contained chaos

My lovers don't complain
but they expect
my offerings deposed neatly
in a coffer of
classified reactions

My lovers don't complain
but I seem to conduct
a poorly orchestrated fugue
an F-sharp major variation
on a tone-deaf diatribe

Unmask

Voracious Sir,
It is a mutual anomaly
That we both claim to be
Serious.
There is no ban on ecstasy
As long as we both play
Delirious.
Vacate the premises of someone's heart
Is tough
But not as rough
As cloning past desires,
For it's no longer human what inspires
Such constancy to repetition.
It's an act of indulgent attrition,
The perverse will to strive
To orbit 'round a Moon that will not jive.
Although we know of its volcanic landscape
Of its beauty's dependence on the sun
We orbit all around and give it credit
It's but a sterile rock that light will edit
And exalt.
It's not our fault
That sometimes what we gaze upon
Reflects but not returns
The love we cradle and expect.
We're light and sound effect,
Director, actors, all
The cast and crew;
That magic show was you applauding you.
And so, shy, lusty Sir, I ask:
Isn't it better to remove the mask
With built-in tunnel vision and refractors?
Why not examine the true factors
Contributing to this impasse?
My point is rather crass
But faithful to my line of thought:
Let's not define each other by the light we give.
Let's sign our pleasure treaty and let live.

December Love

Where is my December love?
the one you predicted
when I walked through Woodstock
naked with yearnings
and pleas
unquestioningly warped
inside my echelons
of mystical architecture

Where is my December love?
you spoke fast
a Tarot keyboard flowing under your
pianist fingers
your voice deep
eyes weaving blue question marks
between the Moon the Hanged Man
2 of cups
7 of pentacles
and my hazel distress

You must have patience
you said
and I dove into the waters of your words
searching for something I did not
already want
to let drown

Where is my December love?
you promised the High Priestess
a King identified
untrapping himself in the twelfth month
the Lovers on the table
my face your open book
charmed codes flying through your fingers
as if you could populate
the labyrinth with exit signs

you were sweet to my arduous muteness
your husky Madame cigarette voice
a gift of words and cards to help me
write myself into another
constellation
but still I write my own sign
only spelled backwards like a cheap parlor trick

Where is my December love?
the one you predicted
when I walked through Woodstock
overdressed in indulgence and Nepalese earrings

Indecision

I haven't yet said good-bye
to this bittersweet lie
of pretend bliss.
I crush my hopes into dust
just to cover the rust
of your kiss.

You cause me to reassign
a degree of divine
to your mess.
You make my atoms surpass
their intangible mass
of nuclear stress.

We are a hazard of choices
deaf to each other's true voices
of greed.
We sing a quartet for two,
two cages in a human zoo
of primal need.

I play roulette on my heart
and you're quoting Descartes
to justify.
You think and therefore you are
but I can't get very far
past "why."

We are a hazard of choices,
deaf to each other's true voices.
We're petrified.
But I haven't yet said good-bye
to this beautifully wry
state of mind.

a year without you

time
bends and folds
upon itself
like a paper airplane
in a perpetual return
to its origins

a year without you

a year of reversed
definitions
when silences blush
more
than words

and thought
is nothing
but a lame excuse
to hold you
deeper

Subtle Love

profound restrained whispery thought
veil of a dream and drop of succor
a tango of the senses and a rose in motion
longing

a question mark in gleaming mirages of the Tarot
a sylph's gossamer threads
haunting and content
in discontentment

heart swooning to envelop to caress to give
all here afloat and drowning
lucent and subtle
Love

Desert Ride

I'm riding through the desert,
the sun is ripping sky
and crashing on my shoulders
like a scorching cry.
It doesn't matter where I start
to count the shades of gold,
I'm sold,
a bargain for my untold heart.
How would I trace
the promise of your silhouette
when every grain of sand is shallow,
when, haunted by your bitter shadow,
my blood flows to the minaret
of ancestral regret?
I get to the oasis
hot and blinded by the space,
every corner of my mind
a portrait of your face.
This spot is new,
the caravans are passing through,
but I cannot quench myself
beyond me and you.

Torrents

torrents of you
taste of devastation
spiced with my inclination
to stretch unfathomable truths

torrents of you
surprise me
in this millisecond
I'd labeled "waterproof"

cut through the darkest velvet
of cosmic nothingness
and tear emptiness to shreds
torrents of you are seeping in slow flow

detachment is a fracture
like an astral cascade
of agonizing rapture
torrents of you invade

Entangled Particles

You and I
deny
all sense of space

entangled particles
two misplaced articles
thousands of miles apart

the slightest alteration of my heart
echoes in you
misunderstood

your every subtle modifying state
predicts my inner fate
one second earlier than its denouement

entangled particles
souls spun from threads of singular consent
one Matter the gods bent and split in two

I
and
You

fed dissonant delusions
vanity and age
like some experiment in rage

what alteration would the heart not face
for its entangled particle to mirror
Love's embrace

Oxygen

the air today
is rarefied and pure
as it must be
at the top of Everest
where every breath
is hungry for the next
and mortals share
the oxygen
of Gods

so it is here
atop the cyber promise
of a tender clue
that every precious particle
of oxygen
for me
is you

Miracle

a cosmic miracle
descended
along the Milky Way

tonight
the light of your existence
cracked the wall

I heard Jupiter call
my name
you came

in brilliance forceful and kind
you touched my mind
and now my heart

captured like a bird with frail wings
it sings
no more of freedom but of love

for it's within the sky of your riveting soul
that I can fly the highest
of all

The Underside of Grass

I walked through grass
bent in sunshine slants,
the way your glances curve when meeting mine,
refracted light, indirect, imprecise,
the way your words undulate meaning,
their blinding blades revealed
only to lure me to their darker side,
that obscured surface kissing ground,
waiting for hungry fingers to be found,
unwound, deciphered in its sunless code.
Translation weaves me into braids of dread,
an ancient sorrow for us both.
You'll always slant and blind your soul as mine,
while I will stir the underside of grass
and beg of it to shine.

Love Me in the Dark

You can love me in the dark
Where obliterated contours
Leap no more in fiery tongues
As we argue to be civil,
To discuss the good, the evil
And some creed, the latest rung
On a ladder of concessions.
After such concealed confessions
At all hours of the year,
After the inauguration
Of a contract's frail defenses
Has implanted in our spirits
Lifeless spawns and harmless focus,
After logical conclusions and desire's listless clergy
Have pronounced a voided pact,
You can love me in the dark.
And beneath the leavened stretches
Of relief and raw caresses
Taste the chartered flesh unchartered.
Such distracted architecture
In this plan where designs blur
Every time a word is gesture
And all afterthoughts concur.
Tender promise, doubt's profusion
In an instant, in a spark,
Serpentine, the call, the fusion
When you love me in the dark.

Alphabet

time sings
torrents of azure melodies burst forth
from this unraveling self
and threads of starlight weave All
letters of your name
inside my heart
my one true Alphabet of love
in need of no other hieroglyphs
but yours
in heaven
in sublime bliss
and
in Love

Golden Bet

Golden, golden woman
Pouring out her light
Into the corners where the night
Stole space inside my head,
Her wisdom spread
As gloriously as a summer sky.
Mother and friend,
You never end
To bridge the rifts between myself and I,
To unify
Faith and surrender in a single smile.
It's been a fascinating while,
And I am closer yet
To the most you have bet
I'll ever be:
Me.

Your Chair Creaked

Your chair creaked
a cricket's song
inside a cloud of smoke.
You sat, your mind at bay,
the dishes silent and
the hour late.
What did you dream of
through the patterned stains
on the small window
to the balcony?

Your inner conversations never heard,
inscribed on yellow walls
in trails of smoke,
your cigarettes,
your lighter,
flowered gown
and silver hair.
Lost in thought
inside your cubicle of culinary wonders,
fragrant beneath
the hardened smoke,
your stories wrapped
around the novels three-times read,
pianist's hands with fingernails long
that never broke.
Your profile,
a riddle left unsolved,
ancient and brave
and modern to the past.

Your chair creaked
and I was soothed in bed
by creaking, movement, life,
your presence nearby,
while stray dogs' barks
traveling to my window,

howled through the summer night:
floor number 8,
floor of soft, quiet love,
and tales whispered
into the yellowed paint,
into the bookcase housing crumbling covers
that cradled all the pages you reread,
your force sustaining peeling walls and minds,
and restless hearts with craving stomachs.

Oh, let me hear your chair creak once more!
To know you near
was to know contentment.
And though I never sought
to peek into the stillness
of your smoke-veiled nights,
today I'd beg the walls
that kept you willing captive,
holding your midnight moments
between their cornering claws,
I'd ask them how they knew you
as only walls can know
the dialects of solitary thoughts.

But only for a moment
until your chair would creak,
your slender fingers
leading another cigarette
to lips that locked your Balchik secrets
and turned to me in smile
each time in sleepless angst, I'd step out of my room
to stand there by your kitchen,
your tiny universe that touched infinity
when your eyes sparkled and you said "my cutie."
Heart's elegance and silver mane and spice,
already in my dream
your chair has creaked
twice.

Woman Rising

I lie burning
and she rises,
rises over me.
Body tower,
body column
of audacity.
Lie in bed,
rotating longings,
look for corners
in the circle.
Lie in bed and
count survival:
one, two, three, four, five, and nine,
woman of nine lives and answers,
woman, live, and memory, die.
I lie crystallized reflecting
faces cloned
at dawn's defiance.
More and more and more
I weather
Songs of misalliance.
Woman rising over woman
burning bridges of Pretend.
I lie soft,
she dictates higher,
woman tower
woman flower
by genetic bend.

Letters Rehab

Thoughts uncurling
around the breathing screen,
a midnight date with words
spun lightly but profound as pulses,
cradling the sinewy, the clogged,
the frozen pathways to the heart.
I rediscover you discovering me
in this suspended time,
a moment dispossessed of future,
mine, yours,
and syllables surrender
to language long abandoned,
a current through the soul,
stirring, creaking, awakened.
The Wheel turns
and paralysis relinquishes its grip,
a haunting, a suppression exposed like an old wound
yet granting renewed meaning to dismantled thoughts,
unharnessed time unfolding and letters pouring out…

Winter Now

The trees
on the slanted white
have winter fingers
playing an invisible piano
of collective harmonies
curled
beneath a cloak
of vibrant stillness.

The trees
on the slanted white
have winter arms
conducting
an orchestra of delicate murmurs
veiled
by the immobility
of pure bliss.

The trees
on the slanted white
bow
towards those who care
to know
what they have always known
since the start of the
performance:

This very moment
in its endless flow
of immaculate falling pearls
is a portrait of tranquil purity
by a master painter
commissioned
by this very moment's
self-importance.

The Now of now

wanted to introduce itself
to Eternity,
carefully adorned
in filigree of white and unvoiced music
for fear that the passers-by
would pass it by.

Like so many other Nows
this Now is elegantly
yearning
for immortality.

Aruban Consequence

Blue-green
bliss flows
in supple silk scarves
around my body
now transparent.
The turquoise fish
see right through me,
swim right through me
like the questions I never ask myself:
Who are you really?
When was the last time
you became water enough
to let *you* go?
Nothing holds firm
in the dance of palm leaves
and ripples.
My mind is liquid,
breezy
or just a bubble of foam
on this sequence of waves
that makes no sense
but owns the secrets
of surrender.

Albena

Why are ladybugs committing
suicide in the Black Sea?
My veiled fingers through the water,
life rafts, acts of charity,
are now full of red, black-speckled
dome-shaped wings in agony.
Water-weighed and wandering-weary,
feeble stretches toward flight,
they lie still, my fingers' length,
carried back to shore and life,
on seashells deposited
underneath a scorching sun.

Water dries, and wing desire
animates them one more time,
yet what siren call so lures
this red, freckled Ulysses,
once again, in flight unhinged,
to abandon shore and shell,
hovering, sunshine on his back,
over darkened, glinting waters?
Thus seduced and shedding life,
one, two, twenty freckled rubies
plunge again to depths unkind.

For this self-appointed savior
in the midst of luring waters,
dotted wings and dotted waves,
aquamarine tomb, a flutter
of a cosmic code unyielding.
Head lies back wet and resigned,
playing God, a troubled task.
And the sky looks down unchanged
on the sea of dotted rubies
and that interfering face,
just a larger dot
aghast.

Why Escape to Andalucía

because it is the land of determined steps and motions
all dripping with flamenco passion and loud, raw-voiced
melisma blossoms of hearts singing; because under that
sun and inside jasmine nights, the murmur of the fountain
is no more than a whisper and the mind hears everything
it has not heard before, the suave beckoning so often
drowned by roar of subways and notification sounds;
because tea is a liquid mosaic that rearranges its own pieces,
petals of Damascus rose and shredded mint and almond slivers
to meet your lips at every sip with a different kiss; because the
streets of the Albayzín give you Istanbul's Bazaar in slices

because the color dances of Moroccan skirts and harem
pants ravish you more than the myrrh and orange blossom
scents drifting through narrow alleys; because in the Alhambra
the filigree of walls and the lace of arches beguile your eyes
and your forbidden touch; because the Giralda's bells spin in
circles as if they would throw themselves out of their tower in
abandon; because the Alcázar Garden in Córdoba is crushed in
sunshine and solitude and simmering fragrance of bitter oranges
at 3:00pm, and you can have it all to yourself, if you dare;
because the Mezquita grips your heart and makes it trace the
curves of its infinite arches forever

because there is such a place as a perfume museum and
the perfumes invite you to tea; because in Granada at the
San Nicolás overview you arrive at an intersection of longing
for things you didn't know you were longing for; because in
Sevilla, summer heat, Guadalquivir breezes, and manzanilla
have signed a pact to make the traveler linger; because time
spends time pampering itself and you, if you let it; because
there is someone else inside you who emerges to walk the
soil of Andalucía, and you know that he or she has always been
a part of you; because you fall in love with the land and with its
version of you and with the very love you carry in your heart

because your senses are courted and your daring loved

July in This Granada

This day has at last softened me and
opened a folder into time, the folder named
despite-your-turmoil-you-are-happy-because-
you-are-here-so-give-it-up-already.

3:30 in the sun with blue at my feet, and
all morning demands and all unanswered
questions stilled. I gave in to the peace that
dared embrace my shadow, invoking a treaty
with Now, the peace that knows how wondering
and planning will dwell here as they will, yet
this afternoon song of watery existence and
bodies with glistening skin and furtive
Aztec glances of a young father still
longing for the freedom of mystery,
the lyrics of this afternoon have won.

Blue ripples, flirting clouds, murmur of foreign
voices, and waters parted by decisive arms,
sun ardent on red tiles and arches,
dreaming of the first, the true Granada, I
say yes to this day that courted me, this
day that lulled my agitations into midsummer
lullabies, bubbles, and a liquid sky smothering
thought in silky waves.

Estuary

Sweep low your marine arms through me, my love,
and rouse this river into tidal stories,
swelling and shy, advancing in retreat,
these waters swinging sweet
caress the ridges of your Neptunian glories.
Your saline currents split this lulling flow
tearing off droplets to deck a fortress marsh,
carving my depths in stinging chemistry,
swallowing longings in a crystal promise.
I yield to marsh and reed and fish whose gills
exhale salty cyphers that make my sweet waves blush,
if blushing were the color of merged floods
whose atoms dance a battle of ionic bonds.
I yield to you, I rise and fall with you,
My honeyed waters no longer unitary,
You've alchemized my shifting river heart.
I am your estuary.

Maria-Cristina Necula is a Romanian-American writer, poet, translator, and singer who was born in Bucharest and immigrated to New York at the age of twelve. She received her B.A. in Language & Culture with a Music minor from Purchase College, and her M.A. in English Studies (Composition & Rhetoric) from Lehman College. She holds a Ph.D. in Comparative Literature from The Graduate Center. Her dissertation-based book, *The Don Carlos Enigma: Variations of Historical Fictions*, was published by Academica Press in 2020. Necula studied classical singing in New York, Bucharest, and at the Universität für Musik und darstellende Kunst in Vienna, and has performed at Weill Recital Hall at Carnegie Hall, Merkin Hall, Florence Gould Hall, and the Westchester Broadway Theatre, among other venues. She has given talks on opera, languages, and literature at The Graduate Center, Baruch, The City College of New York, and UCLA Southland. The journey of writing her first book, *Life in Opera: Truth, Tempo, and Soul* (Amadeus Press, 2009)—a collection of encounters with famed personalities of the opera world—led her to many unexpected experiences, including playing a small part in the French-Austrian miniseries, *Princesse Marie*. Necula speaks and writes in six languages and has earned certificates of proficiency in French from the Sorbonne and in German from the University of Vienna. Her rhymed translation of Molière's comedy *The School For Wives* was performed at Canterbury Christ Church University in England in 2016. In honor of the 20th anniversary of the fall of the Berlin Wall, she was invited to translate, in both French and English, testimonials about Europe by noted international decision-makers, innovators, artists, and more, all collected in the book *Europe à la carte* (éditions le cherche-midi, 2009) to which she also contributed two of her own pieces. A regular contributor to the culture & society website *Woman Around Town* and *Classical Singer* Magazine, she has also been published in *Studies in European Cinema, Das Opernglas,* and *Opera News*. Necula's language skills have given her the opportunity to teach Italian and French to college students and singers at Purchase College, and translate press releases, articles, and reviews for PR firms such as Shuman Associates in New York. In addition, she has gained extensive experience working in the higher education alumni/development and public relations fields for both the SUNY and CUNY systems. In her free time, she enjoys reading, skiing, tennis, hiking, spending time in nature, and traveling. Please visit https://www.mariacristinanecula.com.